Petra Aba Asamoah

Foreword by Albert Ocran

SALES 101

What everyone should know about sales

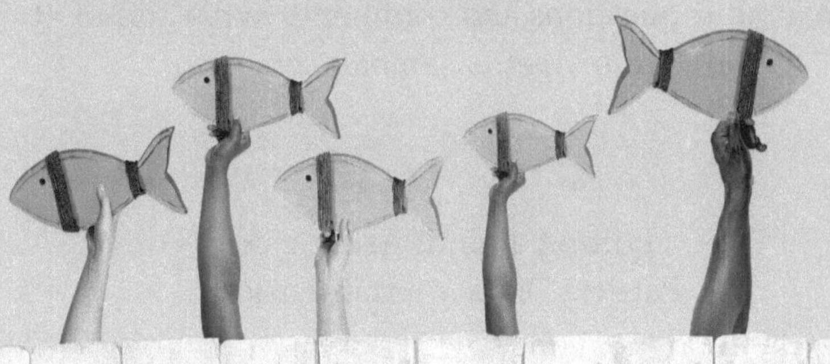

Exemplar Innovations Limited

P.O.BOX 6599 Accra- North, Ghana.

Tel: +233274344000

Email your questions and comments to the author at
info@petraasamoah.com

Editing: Enimil Ashong &
Patricia Dzifa Mensah-Larkai

Cover & Layout Design: Invictüs

ISBN: 978-9988-2-6485-7

DEDICATION

To Sena, Jadon Sena and Joy Aseye – my oasis of peace,
my support and inspiration.

ACKNOWLEDGEMENTS

My heavenly Father, for my journey so far and for the grace to keep pushing – I am grateful.

Sena - my friend and partner. For your friendship, love and support.

Jadon Sena and Joy Aseye – my inspiration, our future.

To my father – the late Dr. Henry Ekow Christian – my first example of persistence.

Mama Gee – my mother and an epitome of determination in simplicity

Regina, Earl, Jasmin – siblings are a blessing.

'Aunt' Selina – your motherly embrace even before we become family, the support you continue to provide is deeply appreciated.

Albert & Comfort Ocran – mentors and friends. Your support, encouragement and guidance has been a blessing

Richard & Najate Akita – this book is a testament of the need for accountability partners. You have been simply great!

To everyone who has supported me on my journey – too numerous to mention, too valuable to forget – I am grateful.

Endorsements

"A fascinating insight on sales, well-articulated by one of the industry's best in Ghana. A good read for current and aspiring sales persons"

Kobby Mensah PhD
University of Ghana Business School, Ghana

"Birthing any vision or being solution driven is not easy, but when one is burdened with the desire to find an answer, solution or overcome an obstacle, the outcome is fueled by a tenacious drive in the face of challenges and turning those very challenges into opportunities. Petra was once frustrated with a sales process that needed addressing. Rather than shy away from that challenge, she has come through with this awesome book, for those who find themselves in the same challenge, to serve as a tool that will equip you for success"

Richard Akita
Life Performance Coach & author

"I enjoyed reading this book; it was very educative, insightful and provides useful guides to navigate the sales sector. This book is a first-hand book for young and upcoming professional. If you want to be successful in your business, I highly recommend this book for you!

Chris Opoku-Agyeman, PhD
University of Akron, Ohio (USA)

"A truly enjoyable read. This is a book not just written or designed for the sales person but a book for all and sundry. The personal experiences shared in the chapters are laced with everyday life experiences. I'd call it personal, gripping, compelling and deeply inspiring"

Jerry John Sena Agbemabiese
Barrister at Law

"Sales and marketing rookies will save themselves a lot of stress by reading this book"

Theo Boateng
General Manager, Laundry Chief

"This book has enlightened me on charisma and confidence and how to use it to my advantage. It is a must-read from someone who has been thrown into the deep ends of the sea and swam back ashore with bruises, but survived it all and is still winning at what she does best, SELLING."

Alfred Ocansey
Award winning Broadcast Journalist and News Anchor

TABLE OF CONTENTS

Dedication — *iii*

Acknowledgements — *iv*

Endorsements — *vi*

Foreword — *xi*

Introduction — *xiv*

----

1. Choice or Chance? — 1

2. Sales and Marketing – Two sides of the same coin — 11

3. All Hail the Queen! — 19

4. A Marathon not a Sprint — 31

5. The Sales Pitch — 39

6. Butterflies & Jitters — 47

7. Handling Objections — 51

8. Account management –With Lots of Love — 57

9. Service Recovery – what to do when
something goes wrong   63

10. Selling responsibly   67

11. Networking and social capital   75

12. The Sell-attitudes: Qualities of
winning sales people   83

13. In the final analysis…   91

References   93

FOREWORD

---

*"Everything you've ever wanted is on the
other side of fear."*

George Addair

If there is one skill literally everyone needs in their careers, it has to be the ability to sell. Whether we know it or not, we are always selling one thing or another. The pastor, the lawyer, the politician, the artist, the chef, the astronaut, the newscaster and the fashion designer are de facto salespeople.

So why do people fear sales so much? Why do we tend to be so paranoid about something we literally do daily? The answer is simple. Many people are unaware of what it takes to be a sales champion in their field. They see sales as the very difficult job of a professional sales department.

That is why this book *Sales 101* by Petra Aba Asamoah is a must read for every professional and anyone with aspirations for a top position in their field. The truth is, as you climb higher in any professional endeavour, your success depends less on your technical ability and more on skills like selling, public speaking, managing people and negotiation, a number of which are treated in this book.

Petra Aba Asamoah is a consummate salesperson. She has the rare distinction of having transitioned successfully from the frontline sales role, through the middle belt of supervision to the executive level of strategy in sales, marketing and customer service. She brings this expanse of experience to bear in this her premier publication which is bound to be the first of many.

Sales 101 has the unique distinction of qualifying both as a sales textbook and as an everyday read for anyone seeking to improve themselves and advance in their careers. The writing style is simple, engaging and compelling. The writer borrows from practical experiences and liberally shares own frustrations and triumphs to help bring home the various lessons.

I tried to single out my favourite chapter in Sales 101 and I will tell you why it was a struggle. The ethical part of me was impressed with "Selling Responsibly" for obvious reasons. "Butterflies and Jitters" are a daily experience for even the most experienced salespersons.

"Overcoming Objections" came across as the chapter that would heal many people's biggest sales fear - rejection. I eventually settled on "A marathon and not a sprint" because it is one of the most powerful laws of progress in any venture in life.

A solid grasp of the foundational sales principles shared in this book will transform your career, increase your confidence and help you to seize your opportunities in life. I wholly and unreservedly recommend this book, *Sales 101*, by my friend Petra Aba Asamoah and prayerfully expect it to be a hugely successful publication.

Rev. Albert Ocran,
Pastor, Author and Executive Coach.

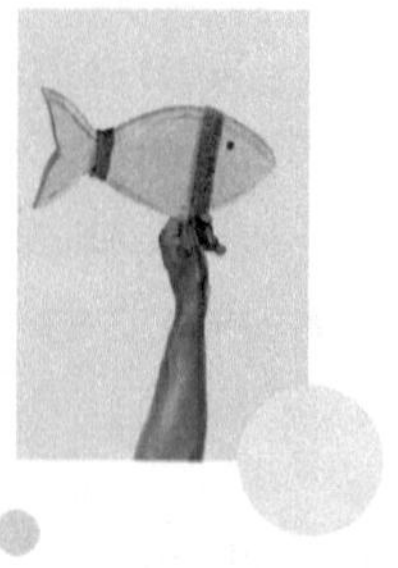

INTRODUCTION

A lot of what I know in sales I learnt the *hard way*. I was given an opportunity in sales after being in a front-line customer service role for two years. I had some great mentors but I still had to learn to become *streetwise*, by doing and failing and trying and succeeding and trying again. My first steps were tough.

One fine day in 2015, I got a call from a lady who was trying to sell something to me. Her confusion and inability to communicate to me why she called, what she wanted, who she was and literally the inability to answer any of my questions, led me to a rant on Facebook about how sales people and sales managers needed to get their act together. I bemoaned the fact that this young woman, aside from not being prepared for this sales call, obviously did not have a clue about the product she wanted to sell to me. A few days later, I had an "eureka" moment. It was not enough to rant, I decided I had to do something about it.

Marketing has received a lot of attention across the globe and particularly in my part of the world, but there is very little skills training in sales.

The easiest thing to do was to start on Facebook. So, I decided I was going to have sales-related discussions by sharing my experience with sales, my struggles and my triumphs. Voilà! *Sales 101* was born! This led to a weekly sales discussion on my Facebook page, focusing on some of the topics you will be coming across in this book.

I have also written blog posts on the issues and these are accessible on my blog – petraasamoah.com. This book is meant to be a foundational tool for beginners starting out in the world of sales but will also prove to be a valuable tool in the hands of the already established sales people on their way to becoming high-earning, world class sales men and women.

When I started out in sales, I wished I could lay hands on a book like this to read, to launch me into the realities of this sphere of the working world, but alas I did not and I had to struggle until I could make meaning of all the tough lessons and bring them into this melting pot, just to make your journey much more enjoyable.

My biggest lesson in sales has been the fact that I have learnt how to handle rejection and not be demotivated by it. I have learnt how to separate – *I-don't-want-to-buy-what-you-are-selling* from *I-don't-like-you-as-a-person*. I have learnt how to separate personal from professional. I realized very quickly that in the business world, some decisions are just the *math*. The confidence and inner resoluteness to move to the next sales call when the just-ended one did not go so well. The strength of mind to keep trying even when the results do not look very promising, but believing that the leads will convert to accounts…as you consistently work your way through the sales process.

This book has been designed to be a *quick reference guide* for you. Especially on those days when you are just trying to figure out – *What should I do?* This book draws on the experiences I have had whilst selling within a corporate, largely business to business (B2B) environment. Interactions with individuals within corporations were done in the context of their influence on the purchase decision. In this book although very little attention is given to retail sales or business to consumer (B2C) scenarios, because the focus is on corporate sales, the experiences shared here can be useful to varied sales scenarios. I therefore agree with Zig Ziglar that we are *all in sales*, so this book will come in handy for anyone trying to sell just about anything - from Apples to Zebras.

I hope you will enjoy reading this book as much as I have enjoyed writing it.

Enjoy the read

CHAPTER ONE

CHOICE OR CHANCE?

"Everyone is in sales"

Zig Ziglar

I did not choose my first sales job and it was not easy; in fact, there were times I hated it. It was very hard. There were those days I did not want to go back to work if it meant having to drive around the city of Accra through traffic, calling on corporate prospects who were always too busy to meet you, when you *did not* have an appointment and sometimes too busy to meet you even when you *did* have an appointment. There were those days you just did not make any progress…seemingly.

I started out as a front desk executive in an airline ticket office and then was moved into the sales and reservations department. Selling airline tickets, a service, as a reservation sales agent over the phone or in person, was easy for me; I was good at being nice. I liked helping my customers make the right choices. I was discovering the world through the routes of various connecting flights and hubs. I interacted with customers and followed up on them to ensure they came by to pay for their tickets. Even when they said they were not going to fly with our carrier, I still managed to remain pleasant and kept in touch for future business.

At my first appraisal, I was asked about my plans. I blurted out what I have now realized was the most ridiculous yet audacious response: I did not think I would be able to stay for more than 2 years in the company because I felt what I was doing was boring. With the benefit of hindsight, I am so grateful to that supervisor who saw beyond my audacity to help me better explore my potential. That conversation ended up being what I needed to switch roles from reservations to sales. That is how I started off in sales. I was excited! I thought I was going to meet more people, and invariably experience more opportunities to use my abilities…and I felt it was going to be more fun. Or so I *thought*. I was in for a rude awakening!

First, I had to send in so many reports – these reports were required daily. I had daily call plan targets. Then, I had to drive for long hours and get lost trying to find my way from one account to the other. The biggest part of my frustration was the length of time and the amount of effort it took for me to close a sale. Unlike being a front-line reservation sales agent, whom customers walked *to* to buy from, this time around I had to go *out* looking for business on my own. No training and no experience… just a willingness to learn and work hard and having lots of hope that I would succeed.

So how did I fare in those first few months? I will say *abysmally*. I had no clear sense of what I was supposed to be doing: and I had become so used to sitting in my office and expecting customers to come to me that it was an extra effort getting out of my comfortable office into the heat of the day…every day. There were days I felt I was just not making any progress: I still did not know what to do. My salvation was a 'revolution' in the company. We went through a difficult patch where everyone had to push extra hard. Our Managing Director got involved in monitoring our sales activities and the sales team was reporting on a weekly basis, aside from the daily reports. Oh, how I dreaded those meetings! I had to present all my prospects for the week and report on the activities of the previous week – to management. I had to report, line-by-line, on everything I was doing and endure many questions about everything. Soon, I began to think about all the possible questions I would be asked and tried to address them in my reports. That did not save me from the avalanche of questions and follow up questions! At that point, I felt *sales* was the other name for *hell* - driving for hours, the heat of the Accra-sun and the numerous one-way streets I was discovering in my city of abode. That is when I learned to appreciate taxi drivers and how they maneuvered through this daily chaos.

There are those who start off in sales because *life* happened to them. For example, in Ghana, the unemployment levels are quite high, so finding a job within one's area of passion or talent can be a herculean task and many are unable to overcome it. There are a good number of them who, when asked what job they are looking for, will respond heartily, "any job". It is not that they do not know what they want to do, which is the case in some instances; they simply want to leave their options open so they do not get disqualified from getting any available opportunity. That explains why we often have many *square pegs in round holes:* we have individuals in customer service who have no clue how to be nice to people, just as we have nurses and teachers who have no compassion at all for the people they have been charged to serve.

This is symptomatic of a society where citizens are focused on survival instead of the full expression of their potentials. Sadly, this is the reality of our situation in Ghana. For instance, when I was coming out of the university, the first thing on my mind was to get a *good* job that paid me well enough to be independent. I no longer had parental support once I completed under graduate education and so within a month of completion, I had taken up internship at an NGO where I received a small stipend. That stipend was enough to keep body and soul together and I had a place to go to every day for five months whilst I waited for my national service posting. There, I learnt a lot about administrative work. I learnt how to manage small projects, respond to letters and to manage an office. I reported to Aunty Juliet, my immediate boss, the Administrative Secretary – a lovely, very experienced lady who was gracious enough to teach me. When I speak of the hardship of looking for a job, and I mean *any* job, I know from first-hand experience, what that means.

One of the earliest sales literature I devoured was *Sales Dogs* by Blair Singer (2002). It was an audio book version that I purchased from a local book shop. I listened to it repeatedly. It was refreshing because it debunked the idea that all sales people had to be 'attack dogs' to be successful. I was trying to discover myself in those early days and for a very long time I focused on how my natural personality and disposition positioned me to succeed in sales. I was also trying to figure out what the gaps in my skills set were, so I could close them. I will briefly recap what I learnt from *Sales Dogs* and encourage you to find a copy of the book (audio book, paper back or e-book).

First, Blair (2002) states that there are five 'breeds' of sales dogs: the tenacious Pitbull, the inquisitive Chihuahua, the Golden Retriever who "nuzzles" a supplier until they are chosen as the supplier of choice, the sophisticated Poodle and the Basset Hound who pushes on at its own pace and establishes credibility. Like personality types, sales dogs differ in their uniqueness and strengths and each 'breed' needs to work to their strengths if they want to succeed. For me, that was like hitting the jackpot! My eyes had been opened! I was not an attack dog. I was not the pushy-go-out and run everyone over type of sales person. I was calm and friendly, knowledgeable and personable. So how was I going to ensure that these traits worked to my benefit and did not end up as disadvantages?

The first step to success in any endeavour is knowing yourself and knowing what you can and cannot do. You must, with all the determination in your arsenal, focus on your strengths to succeed. As Plato said, "Man, know thyself".

Another crucial point I gleaned from *Sales Dogs* is the fact that selling thrives on the natural personality of the sales person. All sales people, like dogs, can be taught the same *tricks* (Blair, 2002). The execution of the trick is what differs from breed to breed. Great training is key to the success of a great team. It becomes crucial to continually engage, train and coach the sales force.

Finally, I discovered the type of breeds I had in my team so I could manage the relationships with my colleagues – as a subordinate as well as in the position of the leader of the pack. The breed I found the hardest to manage was the poodle – the poodle looks wonderful on the outside, is very concerned about their appearance but their biggest weakness is getting results. Poodles are experts at manipulating the perception that they are performing, when they really are not. I used hard core data to manage poodles. The golden retriever is the breed that resonates most with my personality and skills set. The retriever sells through extraordinary customer service and goes to great lengths to grant favours to their customers. The retriever focusses on building long term relationships with customers that yield repeat business and future referrals. The three other breeds are the Pitbull, the chihuahua and the basset hound.

A former colleague and friend – Isaac Fabio Wilson, a chartered accountant who has 'converted' and leads Delta Air Lines' sales efforts in Ghana hit the nail on the head when I interviewed him as part of my work towards putting together this book. He said:

"If you don't sell, nothing gets done: we don't have money to pay rent, we don't have money to pay bills, we don't have money to pay all the other departments. They support but at the end of the day we need the sales people to go out to get people to come, and it's that important. Getting the right people out there in the field is very important and I don't think there is anyone who leaves to chance any part of their livelihood that is most important. Sales is very important and firms need to get the most qualified people rather than merely advertising for just anybody to join the sales team because of the idea that anyone can do sales. The fact that the person can come back with some sale doesn't mean they're doing well or they're doing the right thing. It is when the challenges start coming that you realize that these are people who maybe either got lucky, were at the right place, met the right people at that time or used their connections to pull in the sales. When you have tough times, when competition is tough, that's when you see that these people cannot perform. It's not that their performance is dipping but…it's just that they didn't have *it* in the first place".

Nothing more to add.

Selling is a skill. Even though there are some natural traits that predispose some individuals to being natural sales people, the art of selling must be learnt, practiced and mastered.

Sales 101 started as a solution to a problem I noticed. After my encounter with a young lady who seemed 'lost at sea' trying to sell to me, I decided I was going to do something about it. It started with weekly Facebook discussions to simply discuss sales. I later launched a blog, petraasamoah.com where I write, first about sales and then about a lot of other things that I feel strongly about. Some of those initial blog posts about sales form portions of this book. Through the demands of my work, I struggled to keep up the appointment every Friday and when I changed jobs in January of 2016, it was even more of a challenge. I decided, that *Sales 101* had to evolve into something more sustainable and scalable. Two possibilities – a book and a training module. So here we are, the book! The training module started in April 2017 as a five-module training focusing on the basics of selling.

The chapters of this book are modelled around the content of the training. The idea is that the book should be able to answer as many fundamental sales questions as possible.

Here is a list of frequently asked questions from our Sales 101 training sessions which are addressed in this book:

1. How do I approach a prospective customer for the first time?

2. Who is the right person to approach in the organization?

3. How do I start a conversation?

4. How do I communicate clearly and confidently?

5. How do I build my confidence?

6. How do I get the attention of my prospect?

7. Is it right to make my next move after the first sales call?

8. How do I introduce myself, my company and my product?

9. What are the most important things to talk about when selling?

10. How do you convince a difficult client?

11. How do I handle customers who are not satisfied?

12. How do I close sales?

13. How do I manage sales accounts?

14. How do I negotiate?

15. What goes into prospecting and how do I go about it?

16. How do I book appointments with the key people in the organization?

17. How do I maintain customers once I get them to buy the first time?

18. What is the difference between sales and marketing?

19. How do I get customers who are willing and able to buy?

20. Are customers interested in my business?

21. What are the processes of achieving effective sales?

22. Why is sales so difficult and how can I make it easier?

If you are reading this book, you are looking for answers to these questions. Whilst I am not presenting to you a sales encyclopaedia, you will find a good portion of your questions addressed in this book.

SALES AND MARKETING – TWO SIDES OF THE SAME COIN

"The sales department isn't the whole company, but the whole company better be the sales department"

Philip Kotler

As soon as I got into sales, I began to *swim* in the deep blue sea of confusion. I started to think about how I was going to survive. I did not want to drown. My job was very precious to me. You see, the silver spoon that was in my mouth when I was born, fell out of it along the way. I was on my own – literarily. I had no time to waste. I was living in a rented accommodation which was financed by bank loan. Every month, 40% of my salary was deducted as loan repayment. So, I needed my job and I needed to succeed at it.

I still did not understand the *whys* and the *hows* of sales. I wanted to know and understand what I was doing. My search for knowledge led me to the Chartered Institute of Marketing, UK. I saw a newspaper advert by the local chapter of the institute (Chartered Institute of Marketing Ghana - CIMG), for weekend classes for the Professional Diploma in Marketing module. I enrolled, funded by my employer and was on my way to getting a qualification that in my mind would help me excel in sales and *quickly!* I was wrong. First, there was no short cut to sales success and secondly, there was a difference between *Marketing* and *Selling.* I needed information on how to sell.

I spent the next year studying marketing and make some of the best friends I have in the marketing fraternity to date. We studied together, laughed together and learnt together. But I did not learn how to sell. I learnt what Marketing was. I learnt Marketing Communications, Marketing Research, Marketing Management and Marketing Planning. We focused on how to integrate product, price, place, promotion, processes, physical evidence and people to achieve business success. No one said anything about how to generate a prospect list, qualify that list and how to go to a total stranger and introduce myself. I was not taught how to sell.

I went ahead to complete the qualification and became a chartered marketer. Marketing gave me a *solid basis* to sell. Effective marketing makes selling easy. I was a sales leader with a marketing orientation. I discussed issues at management meetings thinking about them from the customer's perspective whilst watching the profitability of our business. I was concerned about how my team members presented themselves when making their sales calls, the branding, the ambience in our office and even the information we put on the call-hold attendant when a customer called our offices. Marketing was a great start for me. But, there is a difference between marketing and sales.

There have been questions of whether the sales department and the marketing department should be merged or not. I believe that a sales person should have a marketing orientation but a sales person should focus on selling and a marketing person should focus on making the product (or service) sellable for the sales person. They must work together. For instance: Marketing must ensure that the brand is visible to prospective customers by communicating the brand essence and unique selling propositions using the marketing communication mix – advertising, sponsorships, events, public relations, etc. The sales team then negotiates and closes deals. Sales people meet and network – get leads, create and maintain relationships and keep the cash *flowing*. Sales people go *out* to look for customers to sell to. Selling is a skill.

Sales however needs marketing. Marketing people ensure that the position the product has in the mind of the customer (brand positioning) is a positive one, which leads to a purchase decision.

This difference between marketing and sales poses one of the biggest confusions in Ghana, (where I live and work), when it comes to how businesses are run. When marketing is weak, sales obviously becomes a herculean task.

One other very important difference between sales and marketing is that the focus of sales is in the *now* whereas marketing is long term. Sales focusses on closing deals and meeting targets which are set in the present. Marketing focusses on achieving long term goals like brand awareness, positioning and brand loyalty. Sales activities which are carried out with a marketing orientation however are more focused on building relationships and are not simply transactional in nature.

It is my opinion that since the selling function is different from the marketing function, sales people should *not* be called marketers.

Marketing accommodates sales under personal selling, but in unfortunately, marketing training rarely includes sales training and positions it as a skill. The challenge there is, selling is a key function in any business and must be honed to the highest point. How to have a sales conversation, how to close a deal, what steps a sales person must follow in the sales process, etc., cannot be submerged under a marketing plan in a simple manner.

Sales is hard work – and it must be given a lot of focus.

Selling is not forcing a customer to buy what they do not need through deception of the functions of the product or service or pushing schemes that are irresistible. Selling is not harassing a customer until they are fed up and give in just because they want to get you off their backs. Selling is not begging a customer to buy from you because you must meet your targets. *Persuasion* and *coercion* should not be confused to be the same thing. They are not. Whilst *persuasion* is typically convincing a customer to buy, *coercion* depicts the use of undue force and compulsion. For instance, you coerce by threatening harm to a prospective customer if they do not buy what you are selling.

Sales involves a deliberate attempt at communicating the value of a product to a prospect and convincing the prospect based on the perceived value they would derive from making that purchase decision; hence getting them to pay for the product or service.

In my philosophy class, one of my favourite discussions was the one on *fallacies* - inaccurate arguments. Sales people must not appeal to pity in their bid to sell. This technique is typically used by sales people who are unable to sufficiently provide a compelling reason for a purchase. "Please buy, otherwise I'm fired and I really need this job because I am a single father" – this type of argument is faulty because it is built on a faulty premise. That is why it is described as a fallacy.

In response to the question: what *is* sales? Sales Consultant, Leigh Ashton (2015), puts it this way:

"Sales is not about selling. What does that mean – selling is not about selling? It means simply that the art of selling has moved on from the 'always be closing: sell anything to anyone and to hell with the consequences' era."

She goes on further to debunk the notion that selling is about persuading someone to buy. Rather it is a two-way process of questions and answers, information sharing, finding common ground between the buyer and the product and the buyer ultimately deciding based on the match of the product not how persuasive the sales person was. Ouch! This seems to be contrary to popular thinking about selling.

It is time we changed our perception of what selling is, because effectively, we have wrongly assumed that selling is just about convincing and persuading. Whilst being able to convince another person is a crucial part of selling, it is not the main essence of it. The ability to speak well does not directly relate to the ability to sell.

David Ogilvy (2013), one of the foremost entrepreneurs in advertising, who started out as a salesman has compared selling to "military campaigning where we must analyse under two main headings – "attack and defence". The attack strategies will include the tactics to present a case to a prospect, the proposal, the introduction and all that relates to making a pitch. On the other hand, presenting a compelling pitch does not suggest that prospective customers will not have objections, questions or reasons why they do not want to buy from you or use your product or service. The defence strategies include tactics to handle these objections. What do you say when a customer says, "you are just too expensive"? Do you immediately offer a discount or refer to the fact that the competition is offering an inferior product and that is why they may seem lower priced than you? Notice that I did not use the word *cheap*. The issue of pricing can be a dicey one. In some instances, more expensive connotes quality and lower priced may connote inferior quality. Handling objections is a crucial part of the sales process and we will address that in a separate chapter.

Sales without marketing is dangerous. It is mercenary and not sustainable. Sales people who approach sales with the mentality of 'sell and to hell with the consequences' end up with no relationships, no possibility of referrals and a lot of negative word of mouth. On the other hand, marketers who are not sales oriented tend to be laid back, desk-work focused and need to be pushed to think about the commercial value of their activities.

CHAPTER THREE

ALL HAIL THE QUEEN!

"There is only one boss. The customer. And he can fire everybody in the company from the chairman on down, simply by spending his money somewhere else"

Sam Walton

"The customer is king", "The customer is always right", these are phrases which permeate our discourse when we talk about the customer. In this book, I refer to the customer as the *queen*.

Who is a customer?

A customer is a party that receives or consumes products (good or services) and could choose between different products and suppliers. By referring to a customer using the word 'party', the assumption is that a customer may be an individual or a corporate entity. Customers could be internal – colleagues, or external – those who buy. Internal customers are just as important as external customers, in that each member of a team relies on another member to succeed. For this reason, the relationship between and among work colleagues requires a certain amount of cordiality, flow and professionalism.

There are different types of customer transactions defining whether the customer is an individual or a business and whether the buyer is an individual or a business. Below are four of such scenarios:

Business to Business (B2B): In this situation, the commercial relationship is between two businesses, one being the buyer and the other the seller. An example is a company that purchases computer hardware from another company. The individuals who relate in this transaction do so on behalf of their respective companies.

Business to Consumer (B2C): In this situation, the commercial relationship is between a business and an individual consumer. This is the regular, everyday type of situation where individuals purchase products or services from companies. For instance, you are a customer of a bank (an organization).

Consumer to Consumer (C2C): This commercial relationship exists when a consumer (individual) sells items to another individual either directly or through an internet-based platform. eBay, OLX and Tonaton are all internet-based platforms built to support this type of commercial activity. In like manner, if you sold your used car by posting it on Facebook, or directly sold it to a friend or family member, you are engaged in this type of activity.

Consumer to Business (C2B): Though rare, this type of transaction exits when an individual consumer sells to a business entity. The best example of this is when individuals sell to a pawn shop.

Why is the customer important?

For anyone considering starting a business, there are a few factors that must come together to make it come alive – a vision or an idea, the existence of demand, resources (human resource, equipment, etc.), finances and a vison-bearer (or entrepreneur). Businesses are solutions to problems. Whose problem? The customer's of course. The entrepreneur who starts the business and has the vision can decide to sell the business and move on, the idea for the business may evolve into something totally different from what it originally was; location may change, equipment may be modified and the business will still exist, but if there are no customers, that is, no one to buys what is on sale, there will be no business. The customer is the reason for the business. Without her, there is no business.

My favourite quote on the importance of the customer is one attributed to Mahatma Gandhi: "A customer is the most important visitor on our premises. He is not dependent on us. We are dependent on him. He is not an interruption of our work. He is the purpose of it. He is not an outsider of our business. He is part of it. We are not doing him a favour by serving him. He is doing us a favour by giving us the opportunity to do so".

This quote provides, in my estimation, an opportunity for us to test our level of commitment to the customer. I will break it down into components:

A customer is the most important visitor on our premises:

Imagine the President of your nation walked into your office. Your surprise customer could also be one of your most celebrated world icons – Dr Mensa Otabil, Kofi Annan, the Asantehene[1], Bill Gates or Richard Branson. Chances are you will immediately direct all attention to this individual. In some cultures, like mine, the expectation will be to rise in reverence to greet the personality. Well, think of the customer as that important personality who walked in. If any customer enters your premises and there is no acknowledgment of their presence, then

---

[1] The Asantehene is the King of the Ashanti Kingdom in Ghana.

it is safe to say that the customer's importance has not been recognized. The most common indication of this is when a customer walks into an office and meets a service provider speaking on the phone. This could be the front desk executive or a receptionist. To show that you appreciate their presence, it is safe to put the caller on hold for one minute (by rightly indicating to the caller that you would be with them in a moment). Wear a smile, welcome the customer physically before you and indicate to him or her that you would get to them as soon as you are through with the customer on the phone. Oh, and if the call is a private call on office time, it is a good time to end the conversation and get to work! For those who look out for appearances before being nice to a customer, I recommend that you watch the movie, *Pretty Woman*[2].

He is not dependent on us, we are dependent on him:

A business can very easily get complacent when it begins to thrive and start to take customers for granted. Even in health care situations where patients are unable to 'help' themselves, the customer is NOT dependent on the business. Why? Because without the patient, the hospital – the doctors, the nurses and all their staff will not be needed. Think about a hospital in a ghost town? Who needs a hospital where there are no residents and no potentially sick people?

---

[2]*Pretty Woman* is a 1990 American romantic comedy film directed by Garry Marshall from a screenplay by J. F. Lawton. The film stars Richard Gere and Julia Roberts

He is not an interruption on our work, he is the purpose of it:

Consider this scenario. You are busy at work and your desk phone rings. This is a customer contact telephone line. You do not pick up. You do not transfer the call to a colleague; you simply ignore the call because you are busy. Newsflash – that is treating the customer like an interruption on your work. They are the purpose of the business: the reason for it.

He is not an outsider of our business, he is part of it.

Customers are considered as stakeholders of business entities. There is no point stretching this any further, but the customer is part of the business and not an outsider. If this is true, then businesses need to be welcoming and making customers feel important and needed always.

We are not doing him a favour by serving him, he is doing us a favour by giving us the opportunity to do so:

Even the customer who comes back a couple of times still undecided on what she wants to buy is doing us a favour by giving us the opportunity to serve her. One of the most baffling situations I have observed in a customer service environment is where customers are turned away minutes after a business has closed shop. Granted, businesses have hours of operation, but the way a customer is told "sorry, we are closed" goes a long way to either attract or repel them for future sales. Never assume they will return; make sure they do by following up on them.

If the customer is THE business, then we must spend a lot of time getting to know our customer. Who is she? What does she need? How can what we are offering meet her needs? Know her well enough to be able to sell her something she needs (whether the customer is an individual or corporate entity). Being in sales, you may not be in the position to have been part of the product development phase of what you are selling.

Chances are, you were hired to sell something you know very little about or have never tried or experienced. Selling something you have not experienced yourself can be very challenging, but this is the reality of some sales persons. You were not there to defend why a customer will prefer a package or colour and you very likely have nothing to do with how the pricing was set. You were handed something to sell and thrown right onto the stage yet you are required to *perform*. Granted, you were given some orientation on who your customer is, where to find them and how to approach them with what you are selling. Is this enough? Can we generalize and assume that all customers, by our profiling, are the same?

In the context of corporate sales, a lot of research into

who the prospective customer is, considering that each customer is unique (even though there are some similarities), goes a long way to help you the sales person, towards making progress and closing the sale.

During a sales call, you should make it a priority to get to know the customer. Bear in mind, before the actual meeting, you may have made some assumptions based on your research. Take the opportunity to ask the right questions and get some confirmed information on who they are and what they need. The sales call is not mainly to rattle your sales pitch; it is also an opportunity for you to get to know your customer. *Listening* is a skill that a sales person needs to develop. There is a difference between *hearing* and *listening*. You hear when you are the recipient of sound. You *listen* when you pay attention and can recall what you were told. Active listening also requires note-taking. It is not a good idea to rely on your memory. Taking notes comes in handy after the meeting when you are working on the follow up or next steps of the sales call. It gives you a background of each sales call and something to refer to and use in your daily or weekly reports. It's quite annoying for a customer when you should call them after a sales meeting to ask the same questions you already asked during the earlier encounter with them; simply because you had forgotten their responses.

Listening actively also requires that you listen to the unspoken needs of the customer. For instance, if a customer whom you are trying to sell an air travel package to, indicates they will be travelling with their elderly parents, it is a good cue to find out if they will need any kind of assistance during the trip. Be mindful that not all elderly customers travelling by air will need extra assistance (e.g. wheel chair assistance), but do not assume they will not, without asking.

Why is all this important anyway? You already have a product to sell and you know the price and you are ready to make an award-winning pitch to the queen. Brain Davis says, "assumptions are unopened windows that foolish birds fly into, and their broken bodies are evidence gathered too late." Bryan Davis. Never assume you know the customer or what they need. Things are not always how they seem, it is said. Assumptions can be very dangerous. It is always better to seek clarification where you are in doubt. Never assume - Simple.

What is customer buying behaviour?

To be able to sell effectively, we must place the customer and the customer's preferences at the centre of everything that we do. Therefore, understanding the customer, the marketplace and customer needs is the first step towards successful marketing activity and therefore makes selling easier.

What influences consumer and business buying behaviour?

Customers are influenced by culture – their religion, race, where they live and the environment they are exposed to. They are also influenced by social factors like social roles and social status, personal factors like age, life style, personality, occupation and income levels. Businesses are influenced by economic factors, personal factors relating to the individuals who work within the organization, macro and micro environmental factors as well as internal organizational factors like their business model, financial liquidity, etc.

A participant in one of my *Sales 101* training sessions shared a very interesting influencer of how her business customers purchase. It was influenced by the *currency denomination* of the business, she noted. In her narrative, whenever she was pitching to a new business and was made to fill out a vendor/supplier's form, businesses that had their forms denominated in foreign currency were more likely to purchase more from her company. She sold IT software and hardware. She also related this to the specifications of products they preferred, their frequency of purchase and even how easy it was to do business with them!

Participants in the Business Buying Process

It is also equally important to identify the five (5) key personalities or groups of people involved in the business buying process, to determine who you need to meet with, who you need to explain your product usage, etc. to and who must be reached during your sales calls for follow ups. Below are the participants and the roles they play in a B2B purchase decision:

Users are those that will use the product or service

Influencers help define specifications and provide information for evaluating alternatives

Buyers have formal authority to select the supplier and arrange terms of purchase

Deciders have formal or informal power to select and approve final suppliers

Gatekeepers control the flow of information

CHAPTER FOUR

A MARATHON NOT A SPRINT

---

*"Productivity is never an accident. It
is always the result of a commitment to
excellence, intelligent planning, and focused
effort"*

Paul J. Meyer

Being a sales person has taught me a few things – some of them have impacted my personal life tremendously, and enhanced my professional life as well. One of such lessons is that processes are important to growth and success. Following a process also means being patient and not jumping the gun. In sales, when you are hard pressed for time - running against a deadline to achieve targets and simply in a hurry *all* the time, the temptation to want to skip and hop is very real. What I find rewarding as a sales person, is that performance becomes easier when one spends quality time in preparing for the customer.

A process is a sequence of interdependent and linked procedures which at every stage consume one or more resources (employee time, energy, machines, money, etc.) to convert inputs (data, material, parts, etc.) into outputs. These outputs then serve as inputs for the next stage until a known goal or result is reached.

The sales process therefore refers to a sequential series of actions by the salesperson that leads towards the customer taking a desired action and ends with a follow-up to ensure purchase satisfaction.

We will be discussing the sales process in ten steps. The existing literature on sales is replete with different approaches to the steps. I have chosen to go with these ten steps which reflect what my experience has been and my tried and tested approach to selling.

- Prospect
- Qualify
- Connect
- Identify pain points
- Pitch
- Handle Objections
- Proposal

- Close

- Deliver

- Account management - Retaining the customer.

There are separate chapters on the *pitch, closing the sale, handling objections* and *account management.*

Prospecting:

Generating a prospect list is the starting point for a sales person. Like any process, the value of the output is dependent on the value of the input. One of the first computer-related terms I learnt in primary school was GIGO – **G**arbage **I**n, **G**arbage **O**ut. If the prospect list is *garbage,* you are going to have *junk* results. A prospect is a potential customer also known as a **lead.**

To prospect effectively, you need to clearly define the target audience you want to attract. Who is your customer? The more targeted you are with your prospecting the more likely you are to generate contacts who fit the criteria of your ideal client type. A good place to start from in your effort at prospecting is generating a list. The prospect list is the list of potential customers. How do you know who a potential customer is? A good place to start is to look at your **current** customers for the product or service you are selling or those who have bought it in the past. What sets them apart from other prospects? For businesses, you should identify the locations, industries, sizes, and business models for your best customers. On the other hand, for individuals, look at specific demographic information, including age, income, location, and other information. By doing this, you will be able to establish your ideal prospect because the easiest clue is that they are *like* your current customers. What about if you are a Start-up business and have no existing customers? You may be starting from scratch. Consider the need you started your business to meet and then find individuals or organisations who are likely to find value in your solution.

The next step is to build on the list by adding customer contact data – name, title, email address, telephone number of each contact. At this stage, focus on building your list. Below is what your prospect list will look like at the beginning:

No.	Company Name	Industry	Contact Person	Designation	Phone number	Email address
1.	Mansima Savings & Loans Ltd	Banking & Finance	Mansa Anima	Marketing Director		mAnima@mansima.com
2.	Hakuna Real Estate	Real Estate	Louisa Simons	Operations Manager		
3.	Joi Telecoms Ltd.	Telecoms	Joi Amande	CEO		

Qualify:

The next step is to *qualify* the prospect list. Qualifying the list simply means trimming it down to those who are most likely to purchase. You do this by asking questions (of yourself). Take 'budget' for instance, are they likely to be able to afford your product or service? Do they have a need your product or service can meet? Is there a specific period within which they will make a purchase? For instance, if you are a company offering software solutions to companies, you are unlikely to have a list of students (as individuals) on your list except if they are CEOs of start-up ventures that will need your service.

Connect:

You have a list, hurray! The list will not yield anything if you do not 'work it'. You must *connect* with each prospect on your list. You can connect by email, telephone, in person or through social media. Your first contact must be a very good one. How you make that first contact has implications for whether you can move along the sales process or not. Simple advice – be prepared!

Identify Pain Points:

At this point, you need to put yourself in the shoes of the prospect and try to figure out why they should buy what you are offering. Too often, sales people focus on the product features and benefits without being able to link that to a *need*.

Pitch:

This is where you show what you have to offer and how it will benefit *that* prospect. The emphasis is on the word, *'that'*, *because* a generic proposal to every prospect tends not to yield the desired results. You may have a general sense of what your customer needs, but assuming every prospect is the same can be very costly. The pitch should be presented through a medium that fits the prospect. Sometimes you will pitch over a meal or during a meeting. You may have the opportunity to do a PowerPoint presentation but this is not always the case.

Handling Objections:

There are a lot of reasons prospects can come up with *not* to purchase your product or service. In chapter six we discuss a few objections you are likely to encounter and proffer some responses to these objections.

Close the sale:

All the work you have put in so far is directed at one thing – to get the customer to buy. In closing the sale, a lot depends on you, the sales person but simply, at this point in the sales process, ask for the sale. Do not assume anything and do not leave it to the customer to determine. Confidently ask them – would you like to buy? Can you please fill out this request form so we can process your request? Can I please take your order? Remember that a promise to buy is not an indication of a closed sale. That is not to say that you should not trust what the prospect says, but until you have their confirmation or purchase by way of a contract or purchase order (depending on the situation), do not count your chickens as hatched and certainly do not put it in your sales report as 'completed' or 'closed'. Do not forget to thank them, sincerely, when you do make the sale.

Deliver:

When you have closed the sale, the contract is signed, and the customer has agreed to buy - then comes the *moment of truth*: that moment to offer the service or deliver the product. Always endeavour to put your best foot forward and deliver above expectations. There will be instances where everything will not go as planned, but in those instances, there is the service recovery imperative.

Account Management:

Beyond that one-time sale, customer relationships must be managed to ensure a long-term relationship that eventually yields long term benefits to both parties. In chapter eight we focus on this.

CHAPTER FIVE

THE SALES PITCH

"If you know the enemy and know yourself, you need not fear the result of a hundred battles. If you know yourself but not the enemy, for every victory gained you will also suffer a defeat. If you know neither the enemy nor yourself, you will succumb in every battle."

Sun Tzu, The Art of War

Well done! You're at the point that your prospective buyer is ready to hear what you have to offer. This is an opportunity of a lifetime, literally (not every sales person gets to this point with a prospect). Do not waste time with a boring monologue of a pitch and do not let your nervousness get the better of you.

Your sales pitch is the *conversation* you have with a prospective buyer to convince them to exchange money (value) for what you are offering (value). The word 'pitch' was borrowed from the game of baseball where the baseball is thrown by the pitcher to the batter at the beginning of a game. That uni-directional image of a pitcher directing a ball at high speed to a batter is now an obsolete approach to sales pitching. A sales pitch is not an opportunity to reproduce a rehearsed presentation to a prospect, but rather an opportunity to *engage* a prospect. The best pitches are those that involve the customer, listening to them talk or describe their need and the sales person offering solutions. Here are a few tips towards crafting and delivering a winning sales pitch.

Know your product:

You are offering a product or a service to a prospect. Product knowledge is the first step towards getting your pitch off the ground. Being new to the job or the industry will not be a valid excuse. If you want to gain trust and get the customer to hand you their hard-earned money, you better know what you are talking about. Picture this: you have a sales person trying to sell you a packaged deal for a holiday to the Bahamas. You intend to travel with your family – two adults and two children. The package, as advertised will include air tickets, hotel accommodation, a tour and meals. Then you ask the sales person a question: "what is the flying time from Accra to Bahamas and how many transit points will there be, seeing there is no direct flight to my destination". The sales person, nice-looking, pleasant gentleman, looks at you, smiles and says: "ma'am, I do not know, I'll have to check and get back". Ouch! She has spent the past 30 minutes telling you about how a trip to the Bahamas with your family will significantly reduce your stress levels by providing a get-away, provide you an opportunity of quality time with the family and the opportunity to relax, refuel and come back rejuvenated. He went on and on, about the aircraft that flies out of your city, indicating on-demand entertainment, children's meals and a wide range of on-board services that will make the trip with your young children pleasurable. But he forgot to tell you how long this trip will be.

Knowing your product also requires that you know about your competitor and the industry you operate in. This knowledge helps you project in a more compelling manner the value of your product or service. It also provides you a basis to counter possible objections before they are presented.

Know your buyer:

Who is your buyer? Who are the decision makers in the conversation? What are the key issues of consideration? Who are you presenting to and what must you consider? These are questions that will be answered, by you doing your homework and researching your customer.

Let us keep the scenario of the holiday package as the product on offer and the family of four as the prospect. Knowing this family has two young children is a crucial part of the conversation. Travelling with children is not the same as travelling alone or with other adults. A winning sales pitch will take the children into consideration and the unique needs of a family travelling with young children. For instance, you should consider transit times between airports and give an indication of what facilities are available to occupy the little ones during the waiting period. If there is on-demand entertainment on board the flight that provides a wide range of safe content for children, you want to talk about that too! An image of a children's on-board pack – filled with colouring books, crayons and pencils, with a pilot handing over a pair of wings to a child will be another image that will give you a foot in the door of these parents.

Knowing the customer also means knowing their history of purchase. Who have they used as a service provider in your category of business in the past? What was the relationship like? Has the relationship ended? For instance, if their current supplier provides a credit facility of 90 days, your pitch, knowing this is not something you can match, must include an offer to them that addresses this and promises them an alternative. For instance, you may say: We will offer a 30% discount on all your purchases for payments you make within 45 days of invoice. This way, you provide an incentive for them to move their business from their existing supplier. Some very revealing information may also allow you to be measured in your expectations of a business relationship with the prospect. For instance, if the current supplier is the spouse of the managing director, in a situation where cronyism is rife, you may just be preaching to the choir: the account is most likely not to shift – unless you are able to convince, without any shadow of doubt, that they are currently not getting value for money from their current supplier.

Propose to solve a real problem

Every customer has needs and wants. The best sales people are those who can match customer needs to solutions their product or service provides. Marketing, as defined by the Chartered Institute of Marketing, is seeking to identify and anticipate customer needs profitably. This suggests that you are proposing a solution to a need of your customer. You have to directly link what you have on offer to a need they have. Products that are positioned to meet a natural state of felt deprivation are those that win! Think about the queues of Apple customers when there is a new iPhone or apple gadget in the shops. They queue because they *must* get the new gadget and they *must* get it now. According to Abraham Maslow (1943), there is a hierarchy of needs – different levels of needs for people which suggests their life stage. Maslow stated that people are motivated to achieve certain needs at different stages and some needs take precedence over others. When one level is fulfilled, the individual moves to the next level.

The hierarchy of needs theory is a psychological theory marketers borrow to help design products and services to specific target groups and sales people would have the responsibility to match the needs to the people and sell. A further study of this theory will give a sales person more impetus in putting together a winning pitch and approaching a prospect from the perspective of being a solution rather than simply being a cost.

Be ready for objections

You can never anticipate all the possible objections a customer may have, but you can be prepared for a good number of them. Objections are those arguments put forward by a prospect that question you and your product. For instance, in the middle of your presentation (or at the end of it), a customer may ask "Why are you so expensive?" Now, that type of question should not be answered with a mere "we are cheaper than the competition" response: it should be followed by a justification of the pricing using value as the reason. It is just like a prospective employee at a job interview who I asked how much he wanted to be paid. His response on the net amount of salary he expected was quite high and I made that point to him. His response to justify it, however has earned him my respect and a spot on my team! His response was "I believe the value I will be bringing to the team and our output will more than justify the cost you will have to invest in having me on your team". He exuded such a contagious air of confidence in himself and his work, it was just too hard not to catch it.

Be prepared

Be ready. Simply, be ready. If it is going to be a PowerPoint presentation, have your slides ready, edited and set to go. It is tacky to be correcting grammatical errors during a presentation or filling in blanks during the pitch. Worse of all, do not be caught as I experienced once, with a caption "Insert picture here" on the heading of a slide that required a picture but I had forgotten to insert! Presentations should not be too wordy or long. Short, succinct and straight to the point. Anticipate objections and address them in your presentation. Do this in a subtle manner and do not make it too obvious that you know the questions they will ask post-presentation. Being prepared also means be ready for technical failures. Always have a backup: your laptop may decide to crash just when your presentation was about to begin. It is advised that you have a backup always. The document can be saved on an external storage device. Storing online in a cloud-based file or a good old hard copy print out of the presentation always works You may want to consider alternative internet connections if your presentation is dependent on a stable internet connection.

Be positive – go in to nail it!

Be confident that you will do well. Visualizing yourself delivering a clear, coherent pitch is a critical part of delivering a great pitch. Yes, you may be nervous, but decide that you will do well and then go in confidently and nail it! In the next chapter, we discuss how to *manage presentation jitters.*

CHAPTER SIX

BUTTERFLIES & JITTERS

"It always seems impossible until it's done"

Nelson Mandela

This chapter should be useful whether you are a sales person trying to get better at presenting or you are delivering a speech to a graduating class of a local college. I will be using *presentation* here loosely to mean all attempts at public speaking.

After so many 'bouts' of the jitters, I have settled on the position that presentation jitters do not go away...*ever*. That is why I did not use the word *eradicate or obliterate* in my title but rather the word *manage*. You become better at the art of presenting, by managing your nerves and developing into a more confident speaker, through continuous practice.

Whilst discussing this as part of one of my Facebook *Sales 101* sessions, several contributors were surprised I admitted experiencing the jitters – *often*. They assumed that since I speak quite a lot before audiences I should be immune. The truth is, I am not immune - even some of the world's best speakers confess to some levels of anxiety at times. I recommend joining the Toastmasters Club, which focuses on helping Entrepreneurs, Corporate Executives and Professionals who suffer from Glossophobia to overcome their fear of public speaking whilst building confidence to communicate and lead teams effectively.

My *4 Rs* **formula** may help you. They have been very useful to me over the years.

Research

Research provides the basis of a confident, well delivered presentation. Deep knowledge and understanding of the subject matter is the first step towards managing the jitters. If you are pitching to a customer, you should spend some time to research on the prospect – their business, their industry and have some idea of what they need and how your solution can meet their need. This is crucial to you being able to deliver on the content. Knowing what you are talking about adds to your credibility. Research should be meticulous and from various credible sources. There is so much information online that it is almost impossible for anyone to feign ignorance on an issue. However, to be able to deliver on an issue in a remarkable way, your knowledge of it must go beyond a google search the night before. Dig deeper because shallow knowledge is obvious. You must internalize the information. If you have been asked to deliver a presentation on a subject area, the assumption made by your audience, once you begin, is that you are knowledgeable in the area. So, do not disappoint them by not having any real facts to give.

Rehearse

I rehearse (aloud) my presentation, repeatedly. I practice the presentation, time myself, edit my notes several times before the actual *live* performance. That way, I am more comfortable when I go 'live'. You also need this so that you are not fixated on your slides or presentation notes and able to deliver without constantly reading from your speech. I once had a technology malfunction with my tablet whilst delivering a keynote address to a group of university students. The speech had not downloaded properly and internet access was unstable for me to do it again *whilst on stage*! Thanks to my memory, I had to speak without my notes for a few minutes whilst I reached for my printed (hard copy) notes.

Ready

Be ready. Be mentally ready. I think about the presentation and I imagine myself doing well. I tell myself that I am going to be wonderful and I see myself *literally* in my mind's eye, comfortably communicating with my audience. Being ready also means getting to the venue on time and settling in, familiarizing yourself with the technology, the room and meeting people. It helps to connect with members of the audience before you present. You never want to arrive late, unprepared, gasping for air, sweating and dishevelled. That is the formula for how-to-flop-at-a-presentation 101

Relax

Nervousness is obvious to your audience. When you start sweating, stuttering or fumbling, they know you are nervous and it makes them uncomfortable. They want you to hurry up and be done so they can stop observing your nervousness and end your misery. Even when the audience is sympathetic to your plight and understands what you are going through, your content is lost on them. They are focusing so much on your shaky voice that they cannot concentrate on the content of your message. Try to relax just before you start speaking or when you notice you are nervous. Different things work for different people. Find a relaxation technique for yourself that works.

I recommend two of my favourite books on public speaking – *Speak Like A Pro* by Albert and Comfort Ocran and *Talk Like TED* by Carmine Gallo.

CHAPTER SEVEN

HANDLING OBJECTIONS

"An objection is not a rejection it is simply a request for more information"

Bo Bennett

A sales person's ability to handle objections directly affects their ability to close more deals. Objections are the reasons prospective customers raise that could prevent them from making a purchase decision or that have the potential to prolong the sales process. Typically, these objections are verbally expressed to the sales person and therefore can be addressed directly as well. In my experience, being prepared to handle objections by anticipating the possible objections helps me deliver better sales pitches and close more deals. Essentially, this chapter is a discussion on being ready. Here are five of the most common objections you may face whilst selling. Even though these five have been stated, there will always be that one objection you never expected that hits you right in the face! So just be prepared for the unsuspecting question, always.

Price

This is the most common objection you would encounter whilst selling – *Why are you so expensive?* When a prospective customer raises this objection, it is not always about price. In most instances, it is evidence that you may not have communicated enough value to justify your price. It is good to know what your competition is offering, but trying to convince a prospect simply that the price is right is not the best way around this. Rather, show the value your offer presents. Focus on the benefits *to* them and communicate that they will benefit more by choosing you. When you are in a position where you are selling an option that is more expensive than a comparable substitute, it can be very challenging to convince a prospect, but that is why you are in sales! Why should they choose you out of all the options available? Note that higher price does not always communicate better value and lower price does not always communicate best option. There are instances you must show the prospect that going for a lower priced option is going to cost them more, in terms of time *and* money in the long run. What is in it for them? Show your value.

We will get back to you soon

Soon can be the next day, next year or never. The prospect may genuinely mean to get back but may never do so. The responsibility of following up is on the sales person and must never be left to the prospect. This objection may be an indication that your offer is not a priority for them at the moment. They have to consult with other stakeholders or are considering a few options. Whatever the reason is, do not leave it to them: follow up. You could also walk them through the rest of the process to make the order i.e. a virtual close so they know what will happen from this point on. E.g. you could say: "Whilst you are thinking about this, let me walk you through how to complete your order..." You could also ask for a definite time or date when you can follow up.

Send us a proposal

In my experience, this is the easiest quickest way to say – "I don't have time right now or I don't want to listen, let's do this later". Before having an opportunity to discuss their specific needs, sending a proposal means you will be assuming their needs and providing generic solutions. To counter this objection, try to push for some specifics. E.g. "I will be happy to send you a proposal, but in order provide to you with a bespoke option to meet your needs, can we have a quick discussion?"

We have to discuss this with... (other stakeholders and decision makers)

There may be other people involved in making the decision and depending on how many these are and how the organization works, this stage of the conversation can stall the whole process. To counter this, ask to be invited. If you can be present during the next meeting with key stakeholders you are most likely going to be able to sell and answer any questions directly, than having to respond to them through your contact *after* the meeting.

We will like to stick to our current supplier

Changing suppliers is not automatic and prospects may be getting what they require out of their existing relationship. First, do not try to prove to them based on what you perceive as the incompetence of your competitor by bad mouthing them. Focus on your value. This conversation is best handled by converting it into a request for trial. "Consider trying us out as well?" This presents to them the option to use you in *addition* to the current supplier. You may get a very small portion of the budget, but it is a foot in the door anyway. Then you must ensure that you give them the best service they could possibly expect.

No

This is a real objection that you will encounter as a sales person. *No* could be an outright close to the conversation or an indication that you need to provide more evidence of value. Your next action after a "no" should not be to find the closest exit, it should be to find out *why*. There may still be an opportunity in there. There are times when it is really an emphatic no, and you will have to move on; but always leave with an opportunity to communicate in the future. Do not leave angrily or by murmuring. What I would typically say is "Thank you for your time. This is my business card, if you ever have a need in this area or know someone who does, please do call me or pass on my number". You should follow up with a call periodically too, just to keep the communication lines open and to keep you in their mind. The sale may not come from them, but you may just get a very good referral.

Gatekeepers

Gatekeepers are your living, breathing objections. They can deny you access or prolong the sales process. Gatekeepers can also be very useful resources in the sales process. Whether it is the personal assistant to the CEO, the receptionist or the administrator, treat all contacts with them as an opportunity to make them an ally and not the enemy. My approach is to ask for their help instead of telling them what you want to do. For instance, "Kwame, thank you for your time, I'll appreciate your help. I'm trying to get a meeting with your CEO to discuss an opportunity for us to partner your organization. Could you please tell me the best way to go about this?" When people feel important and needed, they tend to be more helpful. You can turn gatekeepers into internal advocates.

ACCOUNT MANAGEMENT – WITH LOTS OF LOVE

"People don't care how much you know until they know how much you care"

Theodore Roosevelt

The customer is the boss and without the customer, there is no business. The relationship a sales person has with a customer is one that is very important and can be likened to thriving friendship. Sometimes it does not feel that way, especially when you are working through the sales process with a very challenging account – you are trying all you can to get it, yet you keep hitting road blocks and then you do!

Just like any other relationship, the relationship between a customer and a sales person requires a lot of hard work. After several follow up calls and meetings, you finally get them to buy what you are selling and are one step closer to hitting your sales targets!

News flash – That is not enough, the transaction must grow. It must grow from that one transaction to a long-term relationship and it is the repeat business, referrals and recommendations that will keep your targets within achievable perspective and your business thriving. This chapter is about account management. Interestingly sales people tend to neglect this aspect of selling once they close a deal and get the cash. Selling with a customer-centric orientation, suggests that sales people move beyond focusing on a transaction and rather striving to build relationships with the customers. That process of maintaining an existing account and nurturing the relationship towards a long term mutually beneficial relationship is *account management.* Now, depending on the product or service on sale, some customers may never repeat a purchase or may do so after a very long period. In scenarios like this, for instance, for high involvement items like purchasing a house or an expensive car, account management exists in the form of after sales service and sales support.

Using the analogy of how you would act when trying to build a very important relationship with a friend, some things are required to manage the account and convert them from a onetime customer to a repeat customer and an ambassador of your business – when you are able to delight the customer after their experience with your service or product. More importantly, you do not want to lose your customers to other *'suitors'*.

One of the biggest pitfalls for long term relationships is that partners begin to take each other for granted. They are used to one another and tend not to pay as much attention to being nice to the other person; at least, not as nice as when they first met. In the context of a love relationship, this can lead to serious cracks in the relationship. Similarly, sales people should never take a customer for granted. You spent a lot of time and effort to get them; hence, you do not want to lose them. The relationship needs to be intentionally maintained. You do that by consistently being what you were that first time. The first 'wow' experience, why they chose you, must continue. Considering the amount of work you put into getting this new customer, you do not want them leaving you because of complacency. Complacency is evident in acts such as forgetting to return a call after several hours of promising to do so or neglecting to call them or sending a note on their special days e.g. birthdays, anniversaries, etc. Worst of all, complacency makes you believe that they will forgive you all the time.

Establishing a measurable, consistent way of following up on your accounts and keeping in touch so you do not rely on memory is a key component of effective account management. The Pareto Principle suggests that 20% of your customers will give you 80% of your revenue. This means that out of every 100 customers, there are those critical 20 who contribute in a significant way to the success of your business and your bottom line.

Those top 20% of your business, whom you must maintain in an extra special way. The top 20% of your business is what is referred to as *key accounts* and they form the crème de la crème of your customer base. You should not rely on your memory to call on them as that can be quite costly to your relationship. Can you imagine trying to keep the dates to follow up on 50 key accounts in your memory? There are varied solutions to this ranging from using simple tools like applications on your mobile device, setting up reminders on your phone online Customer Relationship Management (CRM) software like Salesforce, BaseCRM or ZohoCRM.

These tools help you keep track of your accounts, your relationships (their purchase behaviour), contact information, etc., but they may come at a fee. Whilst the decision to use a CRM solution may not fall within your scope as a sales person, you do have a big role to play in ensuring that you do not lose those accounts you worked so hard to secure for the company. So, if it means using an excel sheet to keep track, then do it!

A simple but important way to make a customer feel special is to remember their name. Recognizing a customer who walks into your premises, greeting them by their name is a great way to say, "I value you". Using words like *sweetie* to refer to your customer can be quite tacky especially if that is your way of masking your inability to remember their name. To some customers, it can be deemed as offensive.

Imagine being in a friendship with someone you never ever communicate with. I've chosen the word 'communicate' deliberately because it has to be a two-way street and not a monologue that has a sales person bombarding the customer with information. In our very fast-paced world, one call you failed to return could mean your customer moving to a competitor. You cannot have a successful relationship with someone if you are incommunicado. Keep the communication lines open. In sales, you must be accessible and responsive, otherwise you lose business. Do all this with lots of love.

Maintaining a thriving relationship also involves activities to retain a customer's confidence when things go wrong. Service recovery is a key part of sales which will be discussed in our next chapter.

CHAPTER NINE

SERVICE RECOVERY – WHAT TO DO WHEN SOMETHING GOES WRONG

Whatever can go wrong will go wrong

Murphy's Law

Sometimes things go wrong. There will be instances when the customer will not be entirely satisfied with your product or service. In some instances, they will be outright dissatisfied. What do you do when something goes wrong or not as *right* as you expected or promised? That is the essence of service recovery.

Christian Grönroos (1990), an academic who has done extensive work in the service marketing field, defined service recovery as "any manner of responses and actions taken by the service provider to resolve problems that arise between customers and organizations". Additionally, A Parasuraman (2006) another thought leader in marketing, explains service recovery as "those actions taken by an organization or service supplier in response to a service failure and the attempt by the firm to correct or minimize the impact of a service failure on a customer".

The *service recovery paradox* suggests that customers may rate performance higher if a delivery failure occurs and the organization and its contact personnel recover from the failure, than if the initial problem did not occur. This is a paradox because naturally, you will expect that a customer who has not experienced a service failure should be a happy camper! But this phenomenon suggests that customers who *have* experienced a service failure and *experienced a successful service recovery attempt are* more satisfied.

There is the 'zero defects' school of thought that has no tolerance for failures and the other side of the divide among practitioners and writers in the service literature that posit that service delivery is 'failure-prone'. I believe service delivery – especially when you are offering an intangible service and not selling a product, is failure-prone.

When something goes wrong, customers tend to respond in a number of predictable ways – complaining, engaging in negative word-of-mouth tactics, communicating openly to management or switching service providers.

The greatest hindrance for service firms in managing service failures and carrying out service recovery, is the propensity of only between five to ten percent of dissatisfied customers going through the process of complaining to announce their dissatisfaction – the majority simply go away never to return or end up dissuading their friends and family from using the service provider.

What *do* you do when something goes wrong? Depending on what happened, who it happened to and when, you could do one of a number of things – explain, apologize or compensate. What you should not do is justify the failure, excuse it away or refuse to accept responsibility as a representative of your company for the service failure. Do not forget, we are talking about the *Queen* here, the boss of the business. If you offended the owner of the organization you work for, especially if you intend to continue to work there and have a healthy working relationship, chances are you will find a way to apologize and regain your boss' confidence. When something goes wrong and the customer is dissatisfied, something needs to be done to remedy the situation. Unfortunately, there are some service failures that cannot be remedied and a sincere apology may just be the only option available.

Whatever you do, do not try to get out of it by lying or passing the buck to the customer. The customer is *queen*.

SELLING RESPONSIBLY

"Being good is good business"

Anita Roddick

To write about responsible selling, it is important I give a bit of context and background to where I live and where I have worked since the beginning of my career. Ghana is in West Africa and considered an oasis of peace. Despite the relative peace and calm, unemployment is a reality. It is very common to meet a young person with a university degree but with no job. The conversation on entrepreneurship has become quite vibrant over the decade but that journey is not one that every young person in my home country is willing or able to venture into. Some with good reason. I have had the occasion to be approached by young people who want employment. When asked "What would you like to do?" the typical answer is "Anything".

That can be a confusing answer but the truth is, a lot of young people (where I live), just want a job, any job. Something that can get them away from home during the day and provide a decent salary at the end of the month so they can be independent. The discussion of what they *really* want to do comes much later. I have established two realities – living in Ghana is one and being faced with the reality of unemployment is the second.

There is also a third reality that every sales person, regardless of geographical location must live with. That is the reality of targets and the possibility of not being able to hit your targets. Sales targets are a motivator for sales people but could also be a source of depression and frustration. Along with your targets, come the not too pleasant reality of a *boss* (not the Queen this time: the boss who you report to).

To compound the already complex context of the life of a sales person, is the harsh reality of competition. There are times where you may not have a direct competitor, as in your being the only one offering a specific service or product and your customer having little to no option than to procure from you. In most cases, the customer has more than one option. Including the option not to buy at all.

Finally, there is the issue of time. We only have 24 hours in a day and we do have to sleep at some point. We have a time constraint on our hands and must manage that effectively during each given working period. How much time do we have available to achieve our goals and exceed them? How much time do we have to make those sales calls and close that deal? How much time until we are *successful?* These are the sales person's realities:

- Targets
- Time constraints
- Competition
- The threat of unemployment (depending on where you live).

When you have the above as your reality, it is human to want to go into a state of thinking that tells you that you should survive at all cost. That is where responsible selling must be discussed. Selling must be done within a certain legal and ethical framework. Selling must be done with the customer in mind. Oh, yes and keeping the target in focus too! When you know your product is *'bad'*, as in not being truly the best solution for a particular customer yet you offer it because you have targets to meet, that is NOT responsible selling.

Responsible selling is ensuring that in your interactions with customers and potential customers, you are mindful of legal requirements, ethical considerations, building trust and eventually, establishing a long-term relationship that leads to repeat business.

I was once asked at a seminar where I was speaking on responsible selling "Have you ever had an experience where you have lost business because you were trying to do what is right?" My response was an emphatic yes! There have been times I have had to give difficult information to a customer that prevented them from proceeding with a purchase. For instance, within the airline ticket sales environment, there could be a great deal on a ticket itinerary which may also be non-refundable and non-changeable. In some instances, they may decide against purchasing on the deal, and with no deal, your pricing may be more expensive than your competitor; so, they move.

Customers will hold you to what you promise.

Sell what has been described in communications to the customer/public – give the customer exactly what you put in your pitch. If your advertising said you will offer a 1-foot sandwich, do not hand them a sandwich which is 11 inches long. That is not what you promised.

The Sample must match the actual – if you provide a sample of what you want to offer, the actual product must be a match or a better version. If, for instance, you are providing a sample of a printed souvenir, the main batch of items should not be presented in a worse state than what you offered as a sample. You cannot trick a customer into choosing you.

Can you imagine buying a gadget that is labelled 'phone' and arriving at home and discovering it has no functionality of a phone – that you cannot receive or make phone calls? You will feel cheated and try to return the gadget, and possibly tell your family and friends on social media.

Knowing you may be racing against time to hit your target for a period may lead you into the temptation of *pushing* your customer to buy and to buy now! My advice is always think about the future. You may win that one sale, but lose the opportunity of a lifelong customer who could potentially be a high net worth customer. Push all the same, sales thrive on persistence. You just have to be measured with who you push and why you are pushing and when you decide to push.

I do not subscribe to the philosophy of *succeed at all cost*. A contributor to my sales 101 discussion on Facebook asked about the use of exaggeration in sales. Below, I share, his question and the responses given.

Question: What do we consider to be a lie when selling to your customer.........I'm asking this because sometimes we "exaggerate" our product in a bid to get the customer to buy.... does that constitute lying? Because the customer realizes that after all it's a normal product. The "exaggeration" here refers to magnifying your product. Is it still a lie? to the sales person s/he is just making it attractive. For instance, I see adverts of sumptuous meals and luxurious seats and treatment of a flight only to buy a ticket and to be told I need to have bought a business class to enjoy that. Meanwhile in the advert, only business class was shown leaving out the economy seats making us believe that's what we going to see on the plane.

Response: Exaggeration is considered a lie. Any time you paint a picture of something you are not or paint it in a way that misrepresents the facts, it's considered lying. Marketing communications must be clear and not aimed at painting the wrong image of a product that is not there. That's why when fares are published in the airline industry, airlines are supposed to state, "fares are inclusive/exclusive of taxes"...so that a $99 fare doesn't attract the customer only for them to appear and be told the 'real' fare is $2000 when taxes are added. When the customer feels cheated, you won't get them back next time. So, even though it'll make you sell, it's not right.

Another aspect of responsible selling relates to the interaction a sales person has with colleagues within their organization. The sales people who turn out to be very competitive. Sales teams must strive to work together to achieve the collective targets. However, in some instances, the competition within the team can become so fierce that sales people may be found undermining their colleagues in a bid to win a sale. That is not responsible selling.

Bad-mouthing a competitor is also not responsible selling. Competitors offer options to a customer but they are not enemies. Projecting the value of what you offer in *comparison* to your competitor is acceptable. However, making statements referring to a competitor in derogatory terms is not considered responsible selling.

There is life after sales…whether you build a career of selling or not, and you do not want to have the reputation of being a "lying sales man or woman".

Is it possible to sell responsibly? Yes. Just be prepared to have some tough moments.

NETWORKING AND SOCIAL CAPITAL

"If you want to go fast, go alone. If you want to go far, go with others"

African Proverb

Turn around and run! Run as fast as you can get back into the car and vanish. You walk into an event with a room full of 'strangers'. Everyone seems to be smiling and having a good time and here you come – feeling invisible. You receive an invitation for an event, a networking opportunity and all you think of is all the reasons why you should not attend but go straight home. My favourite excuse (to myself) was "I already know all those people". I was right: I did know quite a number of the people I met at the corporate events I attended (after a long while), but that was no excuse not to keep attending. There was always a new opportunity to meet someone new or to start the conversation on a potentially new business deal and in some instances, to just have some fun.

The hardest part for me when I started out was walking up to someone and introducing myself. What about if they were not nice? What if they were rude? What if they treated me like I was invisible? Aside from knowing that I needed to make these contacts to progress in my work, I also knew that if I did not attend, my boss would find out and would not have been impressed. Oh, and that bothered me a lot: he way paying me. So, I would go to all these events and at the beginning I really struggled. I was told that I had to "work the room", take as many business cards as possible and meet as many people as possible from one end of the room to the other. I tended to linger in a conversation with a friendly person occasionally before moving to my next 'new friend' but the plan was to meet as many people as possible. I gradually got more comfortable with it.... but it was never easy starting off that first conversation of "Hello, my name is....and I work with...." Especially when you are going to butt into a conversation of a group of people you can see are having a good time.

Then I discovered a good way around the scary part of networking events: arrive on time. Usually the host is present and is meeting guests who arrive on time. You also have the opportunity to settle in and not have to make an entrance when everyone else is already chummy with each other.

Why is networking important to a sales person? Simple – you should be known for what you sell. No one advertises their sales people. They advertise the product or service but the sales person must do the work to get *themselves* out there as a contact person.

What is the point of collecting business cards? What do you do with them? You *establish* contact. No, you do not send them a proposal the morning after: you send them a nice note to say hello and to remind them of who you are and how you met. A proposal comes in much later or maybe never. You do not send proposals to everyone you meet. You send proposals to potential customers: people who need your product or service. You will know by keeping the conversations going. You will know by asking questions. First step is to get acquainted and be associated with what you are selling.

I once hosted an online discussion on Facebook under the auspices of a bank. That discussion was headlined *"Networking or Flirting?"* With the preamble: *Networking does not have to be flirtatious when a man and a woman is involved. Yes, we have what is affectionately called 'woman's charm' but when we are pitching for a contract, seeking higher opportunity or just mingling at an event.... is it Networking or Flirting?*

Below, I share some of the comments and questions from that forum:

Comment: Wow....I have been oblivious...now that I think about it I guess it depends on the individual's mind-set and perceptions. What they call flirting....it pays to be nice but being nice can be misconstrued.... a degree of moral consciousness coupled with a business attitude and nicety will go down well in my kind of network cocktail.

Response from PAA: Indeed! This is so true. I attend a lot of events and I notice that women more than men tend to stick to one corner of the room instead of 'working the room'. You don't have to know anyone in a networking event when you get there, but you must leave after having made the acquaintance of a good number of the people in the room. It's tough depending on your temperament and upbringing, but very important in business.

Comment from PAA: *There's the awkward moment when you arrive at an event and you don't know anyone. The cocktail events are the scariest. Everyone is standing and chatting and you feel like you are the intruder. What do you do? You may feel like running away (I've felt that way many times), but first thing is relaxing...just think, I can do this. Then what I'll usually do, is to go get a drink. I may meet someone at the drinks table. There's nothing more confident than stretching out your hand for a firm handshake, introducing yourself, handing out a business card and starting a conversation. Conversation! You should have a repertoire of issues to be a* *good conversationalist...politics, football, current affairs, your industry, even the weather.*

Comment from PAA: Aside meeting people, it's important you maintain contact. It's not a good idea to only call someone when you need something. A short "hello, it was nice meeting you" email will suffice after the first meeting and the periodic hello is needful. You should try to make contact after a first meeting as soon as possible (24-48 hours) so you're not forgotten.

Comment from PAA: If you know someone who knows someone you want to meet, don't be shy to ask for an introduction.

Question: Hi there Petra!!! 🙂 I find that sending an email after meeting someone at a networking event, really works to keep you in mind. Some people tend to reply those emails but others don't. The responses help you to make a judgement of how the person remembers you, or what impression you created. How do you know that the other person who didn't respond will remember you the next time you meet?!

Response: Hey! There have been times I've not gotten any responses. Interestingly, you may meet up again somewhere else. It then becomes easier when you remember their name to go over and say hello and remind them of where you got to encountered them prior to this recent interaction. Some will (still) not remember and others will be out-rightly cold, but don't worry, just keep at it.

Comment from PAA: You have targets to meet and your boss is breathing down your neck to exceed the targets. That's your job. Your network can work for you, but you don't have to do anything unethical to get results. You can ask for referrals "if you know anyone who needs my product, please give them my number and I'll be happy to assist" works for me a lot. There's opportunity for you in the places you least expect.

Comment: Some guys intentionally use the idea of networking to gain access to unsuspecting ladies.

Response: Very true. Motives and intentions are important in every relationship. Unfortunately, some parties may have wrong intentions.

Often, I have observed that either there are fewer women at networking events or they are huddled up with their friends or colleagues (people they already know). The worst part is where it's a cocktail and you find that a few ladies still found a way to sit. Well, there is the issue of uncomfortable high-heels that makes it near impractical in some instances for a lady to stand for 2 to 3 hours chatting, but there's also the 'I just want to be on my own' syndrome. In both cases, I know how it feels. Let's tackle the shoes first – an issue women can identify with.

It's a good idea to know the type of event you are heading off to. Ask the organizers and have an idea if you are going to be standing or sitting. There is a practical way around surviving the event whilst standing – it's the option of wearing comfortable shoes. You can still go along with your 4-inch stilettos but remember you will be straining yourself quite a bit. A pair of comfortable pumps or kitten heeled shoes will also do just fine. Remember, you are not going to get very far if you are wobbling about with hurting feet. There's a limit to human endurance.

Then there is the issue of 'can-you-please-hurry-up-and-end? I-want-to-go-home-and-no-I-don't-want-to-meet-any-one-so-I'm-sitting-down'. 'I'm-sitting-down-because-I-don't-know-anyone. *Duh!* That's the whole point. You need to meet people. You should mingle and by not taking that one bold step, your actions or inactions could leave you where you started off – point zero. Occasionally, you will have someone walk to you instead (thank God!) and start a conversation, use that as your stepping stone, but try not to cling to that one person throughout the evening. You still should meet as many people as possible – working the room.

You may be asking – what is there to talk about with someone I do not know and have never met? How do I know what is appropriate to discuss? Being a good conversationalist will help you survive multiple networking attempts. You should have a large repertoire of information about a wide range of issues – from global and local politics to international relations, football, current affairs and fashion, entertainment, business and economic trends, tourism and even pets. Gauge for conversations that may be controversial and lead to some discomfort with your new acquaintance. In some societies, conversations around religion, politics or gender can quickly turn into very heated arguments. Unless you are practicing for a debate session the next morning, the idea is to be personable and exciting.

You should also have a good grasp of the city you live in and be able to give your suggestions or comments on where to get what. In other words, there is so much to discuss and you should be ready. You should also have expert level knowledge of your industry. Networking gets easier with practice. Just like learning any other skill, meeting people and striking an acquaintance is a skill you can master.

If you are not getting invited, you could check out events you can 'invite' yourself to, or request for an invitation. Once you start building your network of friends and acquaintances, you will begin to receive information of what is happening where so you can attend. You are a few *people* away from your next closed deal, meet them.

CHAPTER TWELVE

The Sell-Attitudes: Qualities of Winning Sales People

"The only disability in life is a bad attitude"

Scott Hamilton

E very profession requires certain skills to excel. In this chapter, aside from knowing how to sell, these 'sell-attitudes' are extremely important in ensuring you succeed in your sales journey.

Charisma

Having 'charisma' means having a personality that attracts people to you; that makes people like you; that even makes people want to follow you. It is that attraction that you have that makes other people like you. Charisma is exhibited in your confidence, being a good conversationalist, showing and having genuine interest in people amongst others. Even though charisma may come naturally to some people, it can be learned. I have not always been a very 'smiley' person and I am an introvert per personality type. I would naturally want to read a book and be quiet and alone on a regular day and even say I'm shy most times…but I have had to learn new skills and practice and master them because I need to succeed in the world of business.

When you think charisma, I am sure there is someone who comes to your mind with that charismatic personality – that person will do great in sales. If you are the 'running-away-don't-want-to-meet-anyone' type of person, do not worry, you can learn. It can however, be quite strenuous on your personality and you will be exhausted most times operating outside of your natural personality.

Confidence

One of the most common questions during my *Sales 101* training and discussions is the issue of confidence. Sales people have asked, "How do I build confidence?" Confidence comes from within: an inner assurance of self-worth and value. That can be challenging when you are starting out and may not know a lot about what you are selling, who you are selling to or how to go about it. Knowledge, they say, is power, and in sales as well, being knowledgeable about your product, your industry, and your customer puts you in a good place. This is not to say that there are knowledgeable individuals who are *not confident.*

Confidence is importance because when you communicate confidently to a prospect or customer, you generate trust and trust is important for anyone to give you their money. Can you imagine committing your hard-earned cash to a sales person who is not sure about what you will be getting and cannot articulate clearly the benefits of their product?

Drive

Drive is an inner urge to attain a goal, the desire to move head and succeed! To succeed in sales, you need that inner motivation to push. Your sales targets can be the motivation, your bonus can push you, but these are external motivations. To succeed in sales, you need something within yourself that propels you to show up, day after day, even when you are not hitting your targets and makes you want to continue to push. If you are too comfortable in a situation you are likely not to change it. Sales can be a very rocky road. There will be days you do very well, hit and exceed your targets and there will be days you would feel like you are stuck in a rot and going nowhere.

Truth: sales people get paid or have incentives to motivate them to achieve goals, but great sales people are self-motivated. They want to succeed for themselves! They succeed because they want to succeed and have that feeling of "Yes! I did it." I am yet to meet any sales person who thinks sales is easy. I have met sales people who are really thriving, yet they concede it takes a lot of hard work. Drive is also exhibited in being resilient or having *grit*. Resilience is being able to bounce back and retain one's original form after a difficult 'form-altering' situation. You are going to have to toughen up and bounce back. If the door is shut in your face, keep knocking on that door as well as other doors. You simply do not quit!

Discipline

I found this quote from Zig Ziglar (2007), one of my favourite authors: "It was character that got us out of bed, commitment that moved us into action and discipline that enabled us to follow through" Discipline is what makes you do something even when you do not feel like it. Selling requires that you can organize, plan and prioritize. Discipline makes you follow through on your leads and makes you keep pushing until you succeed. Discipline takes practice. Sales people usually work with minimal supervision. You may have a sales team leader who keeps tabs on you and demands reports either manually or through an automated sales performance management system, but to a large extent, a lot will be dependent on you and your discipline to follow through the sales process to convert leads into closed deals.

Critical Thinking for problem solving

I remember my childhood and being asked by my teacher to "put on your thinking cap". We all need to put on our thinking caps to be effective in sales or in any other endeavour, for that matter. The critical thinking path is in 6 steps:

1. Define the problem or opportunity

2. Identify the stakeholder roles and motivations

3. Identify the possible solutions to the problem or opportunity

4. Evaluate the information and data available to you

5. Determine the solution you will pursue

6. Build a persuasive argumentation case to present

Your ability to think through problems critically is a skill you need to win!

Critical thinking is not the same as worrying.

When you are faced with a situation or challenge, take some time to really think through it, you would realize it is usually not as difficult as it seemed the first time.

Leadership

Leadership is a skill. To lead oneself, is however, the most difficult area of leadership a sales person must master. Leading other people is also important, but first let us consider mastering *self.* A sales person even though within a team and possibly reporting to a supervisor, like any other individual who wants to succeed in life, must first learn to lead themselves. Leadership requires discipline, order and a conscious effort to move in a particular direction. The leader must first establish these traits in a personal path before they qualify to lead other people. Leadership – of other people is influence. Being able to move a group of people in a direction is not an automatic benefit or *privilege* of position, it is a process that must be worked at with purposeful action. A leader has the responsibility to cast the vision and move their followers towards the fulfilment of the shared-vision. A leader has the responsibility to make things happen.

As John Maxwell (2011) puts it, "Leadership is cause, everything else is effect". Everything rises and falls on leadership.

A sales person, like any other individual who wants to succeed, must grow into leadership. They may be charismatic and affable; the kind of individual others naturally gravitate towards. Regardless of these natural traits, leadership is a skill that must be cultivated. There are several authors who have written extensively on leadership. There is so much more you can read on this. Leaders are also readers…so make the time to read!

Adaptability

A sales person needs to be adaptable to change and new trends. Everything will not always be comfortable – sometimes things change but can be outside of your scope of control and your ability to adapt. Doing so quickly can determine your success or failure. For instance, a new entrant into your industry will present a new set of challenges to you. You may have enjoyed some position of leadership in your industry and never had to work hard to be ahead, yet suddenly here comes a very compelling competitor and the game is changed – forever. To play effectively, you need a new game plan. You cannot expect to succeed with old tactics in the face of a new contender.

Sales people are not averse to going to strange places and spending the night away from their comfortable beds if that is what it takes to close a deal.

CHAPTER THIRTEEN

IN THE FINAL ANALYSIS...

"I have been impressed with the urgency of doing. Knowing is not enough; we must apply. Being willing is not enough; we must do"

Leonardo da Vinci

Sales is not a walk in the park. It is a skill that you can master – for life. It does not matter what your field of endeavour is, selling is a skill you need. I hope that this book has been helpful to you. In the final analysis however, it will come down to how much sales you are able to deliver and not how many books you have read. So, whilst I am excited you have read this book, I encourage you to practise and act on the things you have read.

I also recommend that you develop *grit.* That attitude that says, "I will not give up, I am sticking with this".

You will win some and you will lose some, but you must get better as you go along.

See you at the top.

REFERENCES

Ashton, L. (2015) *Sales is not about Selling*, https://www.
nasp.com/article/B37B4EC2-D838/sales-is-not-about-
selling.html - Accessed 15th June, 2017.

Gallo, C. (2014). *Talk like TED: the 9 public speaking secrets of
the world's top minds*. Pan Macmillan.

Grönroos, C. (1990). *Service management and marketing:
Managing the moments of truth in service competition*. Jossey-
Bass.

Maxwell, J. C. (2011). *The 360 Degree Leader with Workbook:
Developing Your Influence from Anywhere in the Organization*.
Thomas Nelson Inc.

Ocran, A., & Ocran, C. (2015) *Speak Like A Pro, 10
Commandments of Public Speaking*. Legacy and Legacy Ltd.

Ogilvy, D. (2013). *Ogilvy on advertising*. Vintage.

Parasuraman, A. (2006). Invited Commentary — Modelling Opportunities in Service Recovery and Customer-Managed Interactions. *Marketing Science, 25*(6), 590-593.

Singer, B. (2001). *Rich Dad Advisor's Series®: Sales Dogs: You Do Not Have to Be an Attack Dog to Be Successful in Sales.* Business Plus.

Ziglar, Z. (2007). *Ziglar on selling: The ultimate handbook for the complete sales professional.* Thomas Nelson Inc.

NOTES